Original title:
A Garden Under Glass

Copyright © 2025 Creative Arts Management OÜ
All rights reserved.

Author: Sophia Kingsley
ISBN HARDBACK: 978-1-80581-941-7
ISBN PAPERBACK: 978-1-80581-468-9
ISBN EBOOK: 978-1-80581-941-7

Retreat into Transparency

In a room where vines creep near,
A lettuce whispered, "Have no fear!"
Amidst the clinks of cookie jars,
The tomatoes called, "We're movie stars!"

The herbs insisted on a dance,
Twirling in a veggie trance.
Carrots giggled, bright and round,
While unplanted seeds bounced on the ground.

Lights and Shadows in Bloom

Chasing sunbeams, flowers sway,
"We'll paint the skies!" they yell, hooray!
A sunflower tried to take a selfie,
While slumbering daisies, oh so healthy!

A bug named Stan, with shades so cool,
Said, "Photosynthesis? That's the rule!"
Petals whispered jokes, oh so bright,
In this glass house of pure delight.

Fragrant Reveries

Minty dreams of a jelly bean,
Lavender whispered, "A spa routine!"
In the glass house, scents did flirt,
While rosemary wore a tiny skirt.

Basil wrote a letter, stuck it high,
To the bees buzzing, "Come on by!"
The thyme teased, "Have you heard the news?
Sage is throwing a big ol' snooze!"

Glass Bound Blossoms

In a jungle of pots, thoughts collide,
Cacti challenged each other with pride.
One grand bloom boasted the best style,
"Look at my petals – I am worthwhile!"

Orchids quipped, "We're royalty!"
While ferns giggled, "Just wait and see!"
In this quirky space, laughter's the blend,
Where every leaf has a voice to lend.

Captivating Cultivations

In pots and jars, the plants conspire,
They grow and stretch with leafy fire.
Yet in the night, they plot and scheme,
To reach for bugs and break the dream.

With tiny hats and ribbons bright,
They dance beneath the moon's soft light.
A carrot sings a silly tune,
And laughter echoes 'neath the moon.

Whispers of the Hidden Grove

Deep in the glass, where secrets dwell,
The mint's a thief who rings the bell.
It calls the bees with a wink and cheer,
While daisies gossip, loud and clear.

A sneaky fern wears shades of green,
Pretending to be what it's not seen.
Every leaf has tales to spin,
Of sun and rain and cheeky kin.

Shadows Play in Glass

The shadows dance in silly ways,
As sunbeams prance on lazy days.
A ladybug does the cha-cha slide,
While the weeds giggle, trying to hide.

The cucumbers whisper "Two left feet!"
As waltzing worms compose a beat.
They twirl and twist, a curious sight,
In this bright box, they feel so right.

Seeds of Enclosure

The seeds convene for nightly fun,
To plot world takeovers, one by one.
The radish dreams of fame and flair,
While peas conspire to steal the air.

In whispers soft, they share their schemes,
Of growing tall with lofty dreams.
But as the dawn brings light and cheer,
They split their sides, for laughs they steer.

Charmed Glasshouse

Inside the glass walls, plants giggle and sway,
They whisper sweet secrets in the sun's warm play.
The daisies wear sunglasses, looking quite cool,
While the tulips argue, 'Who's the funnier fool?'

Cacti play cards, with spiky bets on the line,
A rose shares a joke, it's punchline divine.
The breeze joins in, with a tickle and tease,
As laughter erupts from the leaves of the trees.

Translucent Delights

Beneath the bright canopy, a lettuce twirls,
While carrots spin tales, oh how they unfurl!
The radish brings punchlines, oh so rad-y,
And peas rolling on the floor say, 'Life's quite shaddy!'

The glass panes shimmer with giggles galore,
As strawberries dance, looking cute to the core.
Each flower a joker, they jest and they jibe,
Creating a party, no need to subscribe.

Garden of Abstractions

In a surreal patch, the colors collide,
With sunflowers in bow ties, they stand with pride.
The violets juggle, while daisies all cheer,
This whimsical chaos feels wonderfully queer!

The artichokes paint, with greens and with yellows,
And broccoli wears shoes, oh what silly fellows!
The whimsy compounds with each bloom and sprout,
In a world of strange wonders, there's laughter throughout.

Blooms Embraced by Clear Walls

Behind the clear borders, they plot and they scheme,
A peony shouts, 'Let's start a prank team!'
With a wink of a stem, they play tricks on the birds,
As lavender giggles, all tangled in words.

Petunias in pajamas play games of charades,
While zinnias gossip in colorful parades.
With a flick of their petals, they wish to confide,
In this quirky oasis, humor can't hide.

The Crystal Frame

In a box, the plants do sway,
They giggle in their leafy play.
Caught in glass, they munch on light,
Throwing shade by day and night.

Bees wear goggles, in and out,
Blasting tunes, they dance about.
Worms in suits, so neat and fine,
Debate the best on how to dine.

A cactus cracks a prickly joke,
While daisies share a cheap tequila soak.
Sunlight's laughter lights the scene,
Oh, what fun to be so green!

The flowers gossip, oh so bold,
"Who wore that shade of red? So old!"
Petals fling their colors wide,
In this mirthful glassy ride.

Nature's Gentle Embrace

Under glass, we all convene,
Punny plants in a leafy scene.
Mossy mats all plan a prank,
Making snails claim they're a tank.

Frolicking ferns and jokey vines,
Share their secrets, sip on wines.
A rose misheard a gardener's wish,
Now it's singing like a pufferfish!

Raindrops giggle on the panes,
Tickling leaves and playful trains.
Worms in capes, who thought they'd soar,
Roll like turbos on the floor!

The humor flows, it knows no bounds,
In our glassy world, joy abounds.
With roots in laughter, stems that sway,
Come join the fun, it's time to play!

Blooming Within Boundaries

Inside this frame of crystal bright,
Each petal laughs, what a sight!
Succulents strut, all dressed to impress,
In their prickly suits, they're nothing but finesse.

A sunflower boasts of height and might,
While daisies claim they're just as bright.
Critters chat with cheeky flair,
"Is it a garden? Well, who cares?"

The thyme is spicing up the scene,
While mint cracks jokes, just a bit obscene.
In this space of fragile charm,
Friendship blooms without alarm.

Chasing shadows, dancing free,
In this crystal, we all agree,
To live and laugh, beneath the dome,
This silly patch, our little home.

Sanctuary of Shadows

In a jar where whispers play,
The daisies dance at close of day.
Beetles wear their tiny hats,
While gossip flows among the cats.

Lettuce leaves in huddled talks,
Discussing silly squirrel walks.
The sun's a snoozer, soft and round,
As shadows chuckle on the ground.

Reflections in the Flora

Mirrors made of leaves and dew,
Reveal the blooms, a wacky crew.
Tall sunflowers flirt with the bees,
While daisies giggle in the breeze.

Cacti throw hats, oh so spiky,
While worms share jokes, though a bit dicy.
The ferns conspire with the grass,
On whom to tease, and who to pass.

The Enchanted Terrarium

Inside the glass, a world goes wild,
Where every petal's like a child.
Mice play tag on mushroom tops,
While lazy frogs do lazy hops.

Lizards laugh in shades of green,
As petals giggle, quite unseen.
Twinkling lights from jars so bright,
Make shadows dance and skip with fright.

Celestial Embers of Growth

Stars peek in through leafy seams,
A cosmic dance of leafy dreams.
The roses pray to moonlit rays,
As crickets sing in wild ballets.

Plump berries tease the boldest bees,
While pondering life with cultivated ease.
In this realm of green delight,
Even weeds wear crowns by night.

Refined Flora

In a vase where blooms wear hats,
Daisies gossip with fancy spats.
Roses play poker, feeling so bold,
While tulips trade secrets never told.

A sunflower dreams of becoming a star,
Telling squirrels, 'I'll drive a big car!'
With petals like jewels, so shiny and bright,
They dance in the breeze, a whimsical sight.

Delight in Reflection

Reflections wobble in water so clear,
Goldfish throw parties, oh what a cheer!
Lilies wear glasses, looking quite wise,
While frogs get together for karaoke skies.

A butterfly lingers, cracking up jokes,
While dandelions giggle, sprouting like folks.
They paint their petals in hues of delight,
Basking in laughter, from morning to night.

Glass Gardens of the Mind

In the brain's chamber where ideas sprout,
Cacti do yoga, stretching about.
Bonsais giggle, their trunks all a-twist,
Creating the oddest, most humorous list.

Violets debate, oh, what a scene,
Over who's the fairest, a botanical queen.
While mushrooms throw parties, they chant and they sway,
In this glass menagerie where laughter holds sway.

Petals of Reflection

Petals wear mirrors, reflecting the sun,
Making all flowers feel perfectly fun.
Clover plays tricks, like a jester in green,
Saying, 'Life's better with a little routine!'

A merry old rose prances with glee,
Declaring, 'I'm regal, just look at me!'
With every petal, there's joy to unmask,
In this playful world, let's just raise a flask!

Reflections on Velvet Leaves

In the jar, a sprout does whirl,
It dances like a tiny girl.
Each raindrop glimmers, giggles loud,
While worms compete to form a crowd.

The sunbeams peek, they start to snooze,
A beetle sings of funky blues.
Petals wink, and soil holds glee,
What a riot, this symphony!

The Hidden Oasis of Glass

Behind clear walls, the secrets thrive,
Where crickets hop and chives arrive.
A spider spins a disco ball,
While ants hold meetings, oh so small!

With each flutter, a giggle swells,
As flowers whisper juicy tells.
The cucumbers plot world cuisine,
In this fortress of garden dreams!

Charmed Rooted Realms

Roots exchange funny pull-up tricks,
While snails enjoy their limbo flicks.
The sunflowers' heads, they turn in jest,
Claiming they're better than all the rest.

A hopping frog joins in with flair,
Croaking tunes to the joyful air.
Each bud bursts forth with silly cheer,
As laughter echoes, far and near.

Sanctuary of Sun-Kissed Shadows

In shadows cast, the mischief brews,
Daisy confetti spills like news.
Marigolds wear their finest hats,
While bees debate on who makes spats.

A gopher hosts a tea for three,
With rhubarb pie for you and me.
The lizards pose for photo ops,
In this haven where joy never stops!

Solace Beneath the Pane

In a little room of dreams,
Plants gossip like old friends.
Beneath the glass, they plot schemes,
Trading secrets as daylight ends.

A cactus brags, oh so proud,
While the fern just rolls its eyes.
They form a quirky, leafy crowd,
With snickers hidden from the skies.

Sunbeams tickle every leaf,
As shadows dance and giggle too.
The petunias share their grief,
For snails who think they are a zoo!

In this space, let's not forget,
The whispers of a playful breeze.
A tiny spider's web is set,
And there, a gnome bends down to tease.

Eden Encapsulated

Within this glass, the jokes are spry,
Tomatoes tell bad puns at noon.
While roses blush, unable to lie,
As daisies sing a silly tune.

A sunbeam finds a plant in dread,
"Is it hot in here or just me?"
The basil nods; it tilts its head,
"Just don't blame me if I wilt free!"

The violets wear a cheeky grin,
Swapping tales of wandering bees.
And somewhere, lettuce looks chagrined,
For he got caught in winding leaves.

Oh, what a sight—this merry crew,
In hues of jests and jolly shades.
They've mastered the art of fun, it's true,
In this glass realm where laughter pervades.

Prismatic Flora Fantasia

In a world contained, colors collide,
Beneath the dome, it's quite a sight.
Hydrangeas riff with zesty pride,
While sunflowers bask in morning light.

A butterfly steals the show with flair,
Rules with luxury, a diva bold.
Next to her, the ferns whisper, "Where?
Our secrets shared in petals sold!"

Petunias' tales have got some zest,
Of squirrelly antics on the prowl.
While herbs recite their best, no jest,
"Life's an herb, always good for a growl!"

In this tiny world of vibrant glows,
Life thrives with chuckles and delight.
Each petal's dance, a tale that flows,
In this glass case—a comical sight.

Nature's Enclosure

Trapped within a quirky box,
The prickly ones will not behave.
With a rhyme, they tease like fox,
While playing hide and seek, so brave.

Sunny daisies, oh so bright,
Lament their pot's lack of space.
They dream of fields, pure delight,
Instead, they hop in a leafy race.

The orchids wear a snooty air,
Complaining 'bout the lack of air.
"Where's the breeze? It's quite unfair!
We feel like plants stuck in a square!"

Laughter blooms in every square inch,
As roots contend with clever wit.
In this castle, we all clench,
For joy grows here, we must admit.

Whispers of Green Dreams

In a pot where daisies dance,
A worm wears shades, takes a chance.
The sun is sipping lemonade,
While bees create a frothy parade.

Radishes tell jokes to peas,
While lettuce plays a game of tease.
The carrots wear a silly grin,
And dance to tunes the cucumbers spin.

A snail entered a racing game,
He took his time, but it's all the same.
The butterflies are laughing loud,
Making a ruckus, bright and proud.

Through the glass, the chaos shows,
While gardeners chuckle, everyone knows.
Most plants here have a sense of fun,
Turning their leaves to catch the sun.

Fragments of Eden Encased

Beneath the dome, the critters plot,
A radish sings, a tomato's thoughts.
The ivy hiccups on a vine,
As laughter flows like sweet red wine.

In this world of glassy schemes,
Frogs wear hats, and sunshine beams.
A puppy peeks and chases flies,
While mint leaves whisper little lies.

The daisies are a rowdy bunch,
Trading secrets over lunch.
With every leaf, a giggle grows,
In the shade where the wild thyme knows.

As the wind giggles and swirls,
The flowers twirl in colorful swirls.
In here, nonsense reigns supreme,
Each petal blooms the silliest dream.

Secrets Beneath the Crystal Dome

A squirrel once planned a grand parade,
With acorns, nuts, and candy made.
The geraniums, all swayed in time,
Reciting jokes in perfect rhyme.

The bumblebees wear tiny shoes,
While sharing all their zany news.
A gnome keeps track of every feat,
Dancing with mushrooms to the beat.

Sunflowers gossip by the gate,
Making plans for a garden fate.
The daisies chant, 'We won't be shy,
Let's freeze the sun and let it fly!'

Under glass, the laughter spreads,
With happy leaves and silly heads.
Every day, a funny spree,
In this world where plants are free.

The Locket of Petals

One rose had secrets, oh so bold,
It whispered truths from days of old.
The violets giggled, swayed in glee,
Hiding stories of you and me.

In the locket, laughter's caught,
For every tiny flower thought.
The daisies stitched a quilt of jest,
With petals soft, they passed the test.

A mischievous sprout, named Bert,
Could make the toughest cactus flirt.
While sunbeams play their joyful games,
Each sparkle calls out all their names.

With every breath, this glass house sings,
Of silly chases and joyful flings.
In this realm where dreams take flight,
The petals shimmer, oh so bright!

Petals and Light in Harmony

The daisies wear sunglasses tight,
While daisies gossip with delight.
Butterflies dance, oh what a sight,
Flirting with bees in the warm daylight.

The tulips tease the roses near,
"You think you're pretty? We disappear!"
Silly stems, they sway with cheer,
Petals laughing, spreading cheer.

Sunlit Solitude in Enclosure

A gnome dozes off with a wink,
While the moss whispers, "Let's not think!"
The sun's hot rays make the pot shrink,
As lizards on logs laugh and clink.

A cactus jokes, "I'm prickly, see?"
"But I'm just guarding my cup of tea!"
They sip on dew, oh what glee,
In this sunny nook, we're all carefree.

The Tranquil Conservatory

The ferns are hosting a tea party,
Sipping sun with a little hearty.
Pots chuckle while they feel all sharty,
As blooms sway to a tune so hearty.

An alien plant thinks it's quite cool,
Claiming it's the intergalactic jewel!
"You're just a sprout, don't be a fool!"
Chortles erupt, ignoring the rule.

Enchanted Microcosm

In a tiny world, creatures convene,
With whispers shared like a secret bean.
A sunflower spins, feeling quite keen,
While worms pull pranks in grass so green.

The frogs croak loudly, a silly song,
As chaos erupts, can't we all get along?
"Leave my lily pad! Not where you belong!"
But giggles are plenty, it won't be long.

Silhouettes of Serenity

In a room where plants wear shades,
Sunflowers are drenched in lemonade.
Cacti in sandals taking a stroll,
Imagining they're beach-bound, that's their goal.

Pansies gossip in giggling tones,
As daisies dance on their little thrones.
A fern starts cracking jokes so dry,
While orchids chuckle as time flies by.

Lettuce lounges in a sunlit chair,
Sharing dreams of escaping anywhere.
Tulips twirl in a playful chase,
Who knew they had such a wild grace?

But beware the rogue pots' seismic jig,
As they break out into a funky dig.
In this fanciful space where plants do sing,
Life's a riot, in their leafy swing!

Glassy Haven of Blossoms

Amidst the panes, hilarity thrives,
Petunias practicing their high-fives.
A rose with shades sips morning dew,
While violets tease, "I'm brighter than you!"

Chrysanthemums wear hats so ridiculous,
The daisies shout, "Now that's ludicrous!"
A daffodil slips on a marble tile,
Rolling with laughter, oh what a style!

The sunlight winks through the glassy dome,
Mocking the weeds that wish they'd roam.
"Stay put!" commands the thyme with flair,
For they know this place has quite the share.

In this glass retreat, plants play a game,
Of hide and seek, but no one's to blame.
With pots that giggle and leaves that cheer,
A riotous show is always near!

Captured Essence of Flora

In a box where giggles unfold,
Petals whisper secrets bold.
A mint sprig dreams of a dance floor,
While basil spices up the folklore.

A zinnia cracks a worn-out pun,
While orchids plan a punny run.
Each frond tries to out-fun the rest,
But they all agree they're truly blessed.

A lily wears a crown of light,
Prancing proudly, oh what a sight!
The ferns take selfies with a blink,
Captured moments, darned if they stink!

In this world, the fun does arise,
As vines twirl under a kaleidoscope sky.
Each bloom's a jester, each leaf a mate,
Their floral circus never does wait!

The Luminescent Chamber

Inside this chamber, lights do play,
Where plants begin their own cabaret.
The jolly ferns perform a skit,
While daisies giggle, "Bravo! You're a hit!"

A bright pot yells, "I'll juggle some soil!"
While succulents dance, each drop of toil.
They crack up jokes that sprout like seeds,
Leaving the rest in hearty creeds.

The bulbs glow brightly with laughter's song,
As petals sway, they can't go wrong.
A beet's in costume, looking so keen,
"To be or not to be?" they shout with glee.

In this whimsical, shining nook,
Where plants spin out their funny book.
A bubbling scene, where laughter grows,
In this bright room, humor always flows!

Charmed Botanicals

In a pot of whimsy grows,
A cactus wearing fancy clothes.
Daisies dance with jolly glee,
Sipping dew like fancy tea.

Pansies shout with silly cheer,
'We're the life of spring, we hear!'
While tulips giggle in a row,
'Look at us, we steal the show!'

The sun peeks in with playful beams,
Tickling petals, or so it seems.
But watch out for that sly blue jay,
He's plotting mischief day by day.

So come and join this lively scene,
With sprightly blooms that can't be mean.
In this world of plants and fun,
A garden's laughter has begun.

The Silken Sanctuary

In a realm where whispers grow,
Ladybugs put on a show.
A snail in shades, oh what a sight,
Gliding slow, but full of might.

The orchids wear their finest dresses,
While ferns engage in silly messes.
A bumblebee does cha-cha moves,
To impress the blooms that groove.

Sipping nectar with a grin,
Bees confess it's where they've been.
While ivy softly sings a tune,
To butterflies that float like balloons.

In this haven made of dreams,
Nature's laughter brightly gleams.
Here all creatures find their place,
Under silk with cheerful grace.

Fragrant Haven Encased

Inside this glass, a floral joke,
Petunias giggle, can't be folk.
The basil winks with fragrant flair,
While minty leaves play truth or dare.

The sunbeams dance on tilting glass,
With shadows quick, and time does pass.
Thyme whispers secrets to the breeze,
As bees buzz near the snap peas' tease.

A frog in shades plays croaky songs,
While dandelions hum along.
The herbs debate on who's the best,
'Time for a cooking contest!'

In this quirky scented space,
Nature's laughter fills the place.
Come join the fun, don't miss the call,
For flowers know how to enthrall.

Crystal Visions of Nature

Within the glass, a merry show,
Where sunflowers wear hats, oh so low.
The violets gossip with delight,
Under the moon's soft, polished light.

A ladybug lost her little crown,
The daisies chuckle, 'Don't frown now!'
They share a joke with the morning dew,
Each drop a laugh, fresh and new.

A spider spins a web of cheer,
Whispering, 'Life's fun, have no fear!'
The petals twirl in joyous whirl,
For nature's dance is quite the pearl.

So step inside this crystal land,
With flowers dancing hand in hand.
In a world of glass, let laughter soar,
For nature's giggles are never poor.

The Flora Fortress

In a castle made of green,
The leaves plot, unseen.
Gherkins guard the leafy throne,
While daisies laugh in tones of drone.

A snoring fern takes all the space,
While cacti wear a silly face.
The daisies chatter, bold and bright,
Sneaking secrets late at night.

A tulip knight, with oath so grand,
Swears to water, never sand.
His courage wobbles, roots get cold,
As weeds come forth, fierce and bold.

So watch out next time you stroll by,
A fortress grows, oh me, oh my!
Flowers will scheme their grand escape,
From pot and pale and garden drape.

Captured Wilderness

A squirrel in a suit observes,
While plants show off their curves.
The daisies call it quite a show,
As they jump around, stealing the glow.

Inside this pot, what's at stake?
The lettuce plans a great escape.
The chips dip in soil with a grin,
While carrots wager who'll win!

A butterfly dressed like a king,
Proclaims today a party fling.
With flower crowns and roots so stout,
They dance and twirl, and shout, "Let's sprout!"

Amidst the chaos, laughter's heard,
As plants recite the silliest word.
Each leaf a witness to this jest,
In this wild show, they're truly blessed.

Ethereal Elements of Growth

In this realm of glassy light,
Strange plants giggle, quite the sight.
A broccoli suits a deep-fried hat,
While radishes bounce around like that!

With petals prancing, strutting proud,
The herbs form up a laughing crowd.
They twirl like dancers, free and spry,
While lettuce dreams of flying high.

A tiny worm says, "What's my role?"
As flowers sing and take a stroll.
They jive and wiggle, roots in bliss,
A mix-up dance, who could resist?

So if you peek beneath that dome,
Beware, dear friend, you're far from home.
Where weird meets wilder, all will see,
The whimsical point of botany!

Botanical Mirage

In a land where shrubs wear shoes,
And discreetly pick and choose.
Petunias gossip with a sigh,
About who's winning pie in the sky.

Orchids pretend to be quite wise,
As garden gnomes roll their eyes.
A wobbly cactus tells a tale,
Of wild adventures on a snail.

With a jolly weed, mischief gleams,
Spilling dirt and fashion dreams.
Bonsai trees in secret laugh,
At every tiny, goofy gaffe.

Curled in sunlight, blooms collide,
Chasing butterflies as they glide.
In this mirage, so absurd, it's true,
You'll find the flora's laughter stew!

Bottled Blooms and Silent Sunlight

In jars of whimsy, blooms so bright,
They giggle softly in the light.
A cactus dances, pricks its friends,
While daisies plot their pranking ends.

The roses blush with humor's tease,
They prank the bees with faux disease.
Charmed by the glass, they cannot flee,
Imagine them plotting their bold spree.

Lost in a world of sealed delight,
They laugh together, oh, what a sight!
With every drop of sunbeam's glare,
They plot their jailbreak, full of flair.

Oh, bottled blooms, such jesters fair,
In sunlight's lap, without a care.
Their glorious giggles, a fragrant show,
In this quirky haven, mirth just flows.

Enclosed Elegance

Behind clear walls, elegance reigns,
With snickers hidden, mischief gains.
Petunias don their silly hats,
While ferns judge hard, like snooty cats.

The violets gossip, oh, so sly,
While peonies just roll their eyes.
A timid sprout, he dreams of flight,
But twirls a leaf, in pure delight.

The tulips tell of wild escapades,
In tales of sunshine, deftly played.
Sipping on dew, their laughter weaves,
While hosting tea for laughing leaves.

What joy resides in this glassy dome,
Where blooms concoct their tales of home.
A tip of the stem, a wink from the fray,
In enclosed elegance, they dance and play.

Flora in a Prism

In shards of color, laughter gleams,
Petals whisper their goofy dreams.
A lily wears a tutu bright,
While vines are tangled, much to their plight.

Oh, mischief springs from every bright hue,
The tulips play tag, like kids at the zoo.
In the angle of prisms, pranks unfold,
As daisies scheme and the marigolds scold.

The sunshine giggles, a cheeky friend,
Bouncing off glass, its spark never ends.
In this colorful realm, where shadows stretch,
Funny echoes of blooms, together they fetch.

Flora's delight, a prism of cheer,
With jokes so silly, far and near.
In nature's theater, they endlessly shine,
In fluttering laughter, forever entwined.

Serenade of the Shielded Grove

Within the arms of crystal care,
A grove sings softly, unaware.
Orchids sport their shades of glee,
While stems poke fun at all they see.

The ferns whisper jokes so sweet,
As sunbeams twirl in playful heat.
A dandelion dreams of the breeze,
But here he blooms, with humor tease.

A cactus cracks a prickly pun,
While larks outside have all the fun.
The mint gives off a minty snort,
As petals giggle in this sport.

Serenade of the shielded green,
A goofy show, a vibrant scene.
Each leaf and flower finds its groove,
In this hidden nook, they laugh and move.

The Alluring Biome

In a jar where secrets play,
Tiny plants begin to sway.
A snail slips on a pea pod,
Wishing it could be a god.

Sunflowers gossip, roots entwined,
Using gossip that's refined.
A mushroom winks, 'Oh dear, not me!'
Its charm is quite a sight to see!

Bees wear socks and dance with flair,
While ladybugs toss crumbs in air.
Each critter dreams of leafy fame,
In this place, they make their name!

Trapped in glass, yet spirits soar,
All together, they explore.
Cheering plants will start to hum,
In this biome, the laughs will come!

Celestial Garden Haven

In space, the daisies wear space suits,
Sneaking cosmic alien fruits.
Jupiter's beans can't help but bounce,
While Saturn's ringed carrot pounce!

Comets zoom past brightly bloomed,
A cactus dreams of being groomed.
Stars giggle as the moon plants seeds,
With cosmic humor that proceeds.

Meteor showers sprinkle dew,
Roses chatting, giggling too.
A pepper plant plays chess with Mars,
As Venus juggles with fuzzy stars!

Inside this haven, all's a jest,
A whimsical garden at its best.
With laughter echoing through the night,
Aliens join in with pure delight!

Green Whispers in Crystal

In a bubble, greens convene,
Chatting softly, feeling keen.
A froggy prince forgets his role,
Sipping rain from a dainty bowl.

Moss tickles the gnome's small chin,
The flowers giggle, 'Let's begin!'
Ladybugs with tiny hats,
Waltzing with acorns, tip your mats!

A hermit crab joins in the fun,
Playing hide and seek with sun.
The wind whispers with a grin,
"Dance, my dear plants, let's begin!"

Crystal walls reflect their cheer,
While butterflies provide the gear.
In this space of leafy bliss,
Don't miss the chance for such a kiss!

Resplendent Refuge

In this safe and vibrant spot,
The plants bloom, knotting every thought.
A fat tomato sings a note,
While spiders dance, they love to gloat!

Under glass, they share their tales,
Of frosted snows and ocean gales.
The radishes compose a tune,
While peas dressed as trees swoon!

Lettuce laughs at every pun,
As squirrels race beneath the sun.
With roots and vines, they love to play,
In their resplendent, bright ballet!

Every beetle's joke brings cheer,
A lively refuge, loud and clear.
Join the fun, take off your shoe,
In this world, there's joy for you!

The Sheltered Arboretum

In a bubble of green, they grow wide,
Plants whisper tales of their indoor ride.
Fear of frostbite? Not here, it seems,
Just sun-soaked laughs and leafy dreams.

Squirrels in suits, they take tea at noon,
Charmed by the glow of a very fake moon.
Bugs with bow ties show off their best dance,
In this plastic paradise, all take a chance.

Watering cans gossip, spilling the tea,
While weeds gossip softly, just wait and see.
Ferns wear their fronds like a fancy hat,
Pretending to be what they're truly not at.

Cacti complain of a lack of good shade,
While daisies giggle in this grand charade.
The potting soil plots a cheeky prank,
In this whimsical world, all joy we crank!

Glass Dreams and Dappled Light

Under a dome where the sun always beams,
Plants party hardy, or so it seems.
A cactus wears shades, feeling quite bold,
While hardy geraniums tease the marigolds.

Bees in bowler hats, buzzing around,
Once wilted leaves now twirl off the ground.
Ladybugs ready for a waltz or two,
In this warm spot where dreams come true.

Lettuce lounges, while tomatoes jest,
The carrots play tag, they're simply the best.
Through glass panes, laughter escapes in bursts,
Tickled by sunlight, we quench our thirsts.

With every new bloom, the giggles grow wide,
In this lively estate, pests take their pride.
Nature's own sitcom, made just for fun,
Underneath glass, we bask in the sun!

Nature's Sanctuary

In a bubble world where the veggies unite,
The radishes rave and sing through the night.
Spinach spins tales no one can outshine,
While thyme tells secrets, all sweet and divine.

Potatoes in tuxes, they prune and they pose,
While herbs plot pranks on the garden hose.
A comical sight, the greenhouse brigade,
Who knew being planted could be this well played?

Leafy laughter echoes, tickling the air,
While sunflowers gossip, a curious pair.
They lean in close, and they share a wise word,
In this vibrant space, no one ends up blurred.

Hoping for blooms that will tickle the nose,
Clouds drift by teasing, "When do we doze?"
Under glass roofs where the silliness stirs,
We find joy in the quirks of our garden blurs!

Spirits in Stunning Simplicity

Among the glass walls where wild things reside,
Lettuce played judge, with peas by their side.
Tiny green ghosts float in playful delight,
In a maze of green under shimmering light.

Friends in bright pots boast of their growth,
While ferns hold a talent show, bringing forth.
The carrots can sing—well, sort of, they try,
In this goofy abode, their spirits fly high.

Orchids don capes, thinking they're grand,
While basil and mint form a leafy band.
They dance in the breeze, enchanting the air,
Creating a symphony beyond compare.

In this whimsical realm where whimsy is king,
Joy drips like dew on each flourishing thing.
Spirits among us, in simple attire,
We giggle and grow, as we reach for the fire!

Fragrant Fantasies in a Bubble

In a pot where cacti giggle,
And daisies play a tricky jiggle,
The sun laughs at the snails' parade,
While daisies throw shade at a merry charade.

Tiny weeds in bowler hats,
Hold tea parties with busy gnats.
A fern insists it can dance the tango,
But only ends up with a sprightly mango.

Blossoms wear glasses, so hipster-chic,
While roses gossip about the last peak.
A talking daffodil who's quite the show,
Declares, "I'm blooming, let's go with the flow!"

Within this realm of silly delight,
Where everything giggles, and no one takes flight.
A polka-dotted butterfly flutters and sways,
As we chuckle along in these funny ways.

Sheltered Echoes of Nature

Under a dome where shadows dance,
Trees debate their favorite romance.
A squirrel claims he's a master of rap,
While critters all gather, a whimsical map.

The mushrooms are in a candid affair,
Discussing their dreams of becoming rare air.
Hydrangeas shimmer like disco balls,
While ferns gossip loud, sticking to the walls.

In this playful nook where plants delight,
A buzzing bee sings into the night.
The vines twist and plot a comical scheme,
As laughter escapes like a daydream.

With every petal that giggles away,
Nature's lost in her own fun play.
Echoes bounce, a raucous clatter,
In this quirky space where nothing's the matter.

The Enigmatic Herbarium

Inside the glass, aromas blend,
Petunia whispers a joke to a friend.
Thyme has a knack for tricky puns,
While basil struts, claiming he runs the sun.

Cacti wear hats, like old wise men,
Who tell tales of when they were ten.
A lily aims to be a stage star,
But gets interrupted by a nearby jar.

Herbs huddle close, sharing sly grins,
Debating who will spark the next spins.
A wiggly worm is manning the bar,
Crafting cocktails in his own bizarre.

Giggling roots and dancing shoots,
In this flurry of whimsical toots.
Each moment brings laughter and cheer,
In our secret realm, a world without fear.

Tamed Wilderness Beneath Canopy

Under the dome where shadows play,
Loose leaves make a bed for the day.
A weeping willow tells tales of woe,
While daisies plan a grand show.

The broccoli strikes poses by the peas,
Claiming they're kings with downy knees.
A chorus of lilies breaks out in song,
As the daisies applaud, "You can't go wrong!"

Raccoons host a picnic with cupcakes galore,
Beware the ants who'll settle the score.
With thistle and charm, they pop all the fun,
In laughter-filled whispers, their battles get spun.

Here every sprout has a story unique,
Of mischief and hijinks, the playful cheek.
Beneath the glass where wild dreams thrive,
Silly moments make nature come alive!

Glistening Dreams in Green

In the nook where sunlight bends,
Tiny gnomes make their amends.
They argue about the best herb,
While the cat, in mirth, doth disturb.

Peppers bouncing on their stems,
Wondering who'll win the gems.
A trowel winks with crafty glee,
As earthworms dance quite merrily.

Squirrels critique the flower's stance,
While butterflies swirl in a trance.
With pots of gold and soil so rich,
Life in this nook is quite the pitch!

The Verdant Vault

Behind the glass, a world unfolds,
Where broccoli shares tales, bold.
While peas play cards with dandelions,
In a riot of green, no maligns.

A no-show snail, the punchline came,
He just couldn't find his aim!
While ferns chuckle in the light,
Basking in their leafy height.

The gardener glances with a grin,
As daisies argue who will win.
With raucous laughter in the air,
This hidden realm has flair to spare!

Sanctuary of Glass

In this glass abode, fun does bloom,
Where herbs conspire to grow in gloom.
Thyme leads a plot against the pests,
With rosemary backing all their quests.

A mischievous fern tickles a snail,
While radishes spin a tall tale.
The sunbeams giggle on green backs,
Bouncing light off bug and cracks.

Potted plants hold secret pranks,
Plotting to fool the cautious flanks.
With every sprout and leafy jest,
They claim this space as the very best!

Under the Radiant Surface

Where glass meets soil, laughter spills,
Among the roots, the whimsy thrills.
Potatoes peek from their cozy beds,
And carrots talk of olden threads.

Chickens wearing goggles, oh what a sight,
Hatching plans in the morning light.
While bees give salsa lessons, dance,
In this bright space of funny chance.

Petunias wear their finest hats,
While peas prance about like acrobats.
Oh what folly, under the gleam,
In this abode where plants dream and scheme!

Spheres of Serenity

In spheres so round, the plants play hide,
Little critters bounce and glide.
A snail in shades, takes a grand stroll,
While mischief reigns, that's the goal!

Tiny faeries lift the lid,
They giggle softly, 'What a bid!'
With laughter sweet, they stir the air,
In this clear dome, there's joy to spare!

A flower's dance, a sly little tease,
The sunbeams twirl with such great ease.
In this tight space, oh what a sight,
Even weeds wear outfits bright!

So gather round, enjoy the show,
Where every bloom steals the glow.
In wobbly pots and tangled spree,
Nature's jests are wild and free!

Bouquets in a Bubble

A bubble forms, the blooms awake,
With frothy tops, they start to shake.
Roses wear hats, violets prance,
In this round space, they love to dance!

Sunflowers shout, 'I'm king today!'
While daisies laugh and twist away.
A bumblebee buzzes, thinking he's slick,
But trips on a stem, oh what a trick!

The tulips joke, 'We're here to stay!'
While marigolds cheer in bright array.
With petals soft and fragrance bold,
Each little whisper is pure gold!

In this greenhouse, giggles abound,
Where playful blooms are always found.
So join the fun, no need to frown,
This bubble blooms, a colorful crown!

The Mustard Seed's Refuge

In a cozy nook, where secrets dwell,
A mustard seed spins its tale to tell.
It stretches out, dreaming of grace,
While gnomes conspire to steal its place!

A worm pops up, 'What's the fuss?'
With leafy snacks, they sit and discuss.
Tiny issues, oh so grand,
'Who ate my roots?' a crowded land!

Through tangled vines, the laughter flows,
As mischief blooms in rows and rows.
With every sprout, a jest is shared,
In this green home, no heart is spared!

So tiptoe here, and keep it light,
Where seeds of joy take joyful flight.
In this small world, the fun won't cease,
Each little plant finds sweet release!

Petals Quivered by Glass

Beneath the dome, adventures thrive,
Petals quiver as critters arrive.
A spider spins tales, tangled and neat,
While ladybugs tap on daisy's seat!

The lilies gossip, 'Who wore it best?'
While tulips pose, they're all dressed!
With bubbles of laughter, they twirl around,
In this crystal realm, joy's profound!

A butterfly flutters, caught in the flare,
Doing a dance, oh what a scare!
These little mishaps, so funny and sweet,
Turn every day into a treat!

So come and see, in laughter dressed,
Where petals play and never rest.
In this clear space, fun takes the lead,
A joyful place, where hearts are freed!

Reflections of a Fabled Flora

In a dome of dreams, blooms do prance,
Wiggling their stems in a awkward dance.
A rose wore sneakers, a daisy a hat,
Mimicking sunbeams—imagine that!

A tulip tells jokes, quite the rib-tickler,
While daisies sip tea, getting a snicker.
The pansies form bands, with petals that shine,
Creating hilarity, oh so divine!

As shadows cast giggles on leaves that will sway,
The ferns roll their eyes, they just want to play.
'No more of this laughing!' a cactus will shout,
But the laughter of blooms swirls them all about!

Under glass, their pranks are a sight to behold,
Stories of sunshine, in sunshine retold.
With every fourth giggle, the glass seems to bend,
In a world where the plants are the very best friends.

Crystal Veil of Blooming Hues

With a wink and a blush, the flowers unite,
Wearing gowns of color, oh what a sight!
Lilies in legwarmers, daffodils cheer,
They dance in their spots, full of good cheer!

Petals with patterns, it's quite a parade,
The violets are gossiping, oh what a charade!
The tulips spin tales of their travels afar,
While the pansies debate who's the brightest star!

Giggling willys, the herbs make a scene,
Sage in a tux, looking sharp and serene.
'We like to be wild!' they loudly exclaim,
Yet in this fine glass, they just can't be tame!

With a wink at the sun, they strut and they sway,
Perennials plotting their next grand ballet.
A riot of laughter under this dome,
In this wild oasis, they feel right at home.

Hidden Eden

Beneath the clear dome, mischief does sing,
Where each leafy creature feels like a king.
A snapdragon's prank unfolds with a twist,
As blossoms conspire, nobody's missed!

The petunias argue, their colors collide,
'It's not just a phase!' the bright rascals cried.
While sunflowers strain to keep track of time,
Their giggles and jests are simply sublime!

The mint sneezes loud, one might call it blush,
Basil plays coy, causing quite the hush.
With every good laugh, a new bloom appears,
In this hidden world, the joy is sincere!

When moonlight bathes leaves, a faint shimmer calls,
To garden shenanigans within glassy walls.
In this secret delight, good humor is blent,
It's life's little jests that the blooms represent!

Fragments of Light

In this bright chamber, the colors collide,
A rose tells tall tales, with petals of pride.
Dandelions giggle, embracing the breeze,
While marigolds match in a jest-filled tease!

They're casting reflections in crystalline beams,
Spinning around like unvoiced dreams.
Sweet peas compose notes, serenading the air,
While the violets blush, tangled in flair!

The breezes are chuckling as shadows play tag,
With lilacs composed in a ruffled swag.
A riot of laughter, beneath skies of glass,
In this vibrant voyage, no moment will pass!

So here in the shimmer, beneath radiant hues,
The flora reminds us, life's full of cues.
From quirky reflections, hilarity dances,
With every light flicker, it sparkles and prances!

Petals in Prism

In a bowl of sunshine bright,
Petals dance with sheer delight,
Butterflies in full-time flight,
Sipping nectar, quite the sight!

A bee in stripes, it wears a frown,
Thinking, "Why's this flower down?"
It buzzes here, it buzzes there,
Confused by all that flowery flair!

Garden gnomes under the sun,
Playing tag, oh what a run!
With their hats, so tall and wide,
Laughing with the blooms beside.

But wait, what's that? A loud clatter!
A squirrel spills a bowl of batter,
Making muffins, what a jest,
In this glassy haven, we're blessed!

Treasures Behind Transparent Walls

Behind the glass, a hidden quest,
Rabbits hop, oh what a jest!
Searching for that golden treat,
Carrot cakes and greens to meet!

A snail who thinks he's ultra-fast,
Sprints by in a sluggish blast,
While ants hold tennis matches there,
And cheer each point with fervent flair!

Frogs in tuxedos play charades,
Hopping high in fancy parades,
With lizards doing stand-up shows,
The glass confines do host their pros!

Gnomes detailing their sweet escapes,
Plan mischief with bizarre capes,
In this bright world where laughter reigns,
Life is sweet, despite the pains!

Echoes of the Wild

Under the dome, whispers float,
A parrot thinks it's quite a goat,
Hollering tunes, he steals the scene,
While iguanas prance, oh so keen!

Crickets chirp their greatest hits,
With fireflies who do backflips,
The shrubs are swaying to the beat,
In this glass palace, what a feat!

A turtle in a mini-car,
Drives around, oh what a star!
Chasing shadows, grinning wide,
Joyful creatures by his side!

The echo lingers, soft and sweet,
Nature's giggles, can't be beat,
In this bright realm, laughter flows,
And wild surprises come in droves!

Nature's Enigma

Inside this glass, a secret maze,
Where cheeky critters love to play,
A wabbit dons a monocle grand,
Sipping tea from a leafy hand!

The tiny frogs wear tiny shoes,
Dancing madly in bright hues,
While butterflies exchange their tips,
On perfect leaps and happy zips!

Oh, what's that? A wind-up worm,
Thinking it's all about the charm,
Wiggling with utmost delight,
Then falling off a mushroom height!

In this world of funny strife,
Nature spins a jester's life,
Behind the glass, where laughter flies,
Joyful antics, a sweet surprise!

Shards of Green Serenity

In a jar of joy, plants grow wild,
Little leaves dance, oh so styled.
A fern's wiggle, a sprout's big grin,
Who knew the plant life could be such a win?

Beneath the dome, sprites take a turn,
They juggle pots and toss up a fern.
With soil in their hair, they look quite swell,
A green-thumbed circus, who could tell?

A cactus sighs, it's got no space,
"Too prickly for hugs!" it says with grace.
Basil's bad jokes make thyme feel sore,
But when it gets spicy, they always want more.

In this playful nook, the animals peek,
Worms in tuxedos, a majestic cheek.
With each new sprout, a giggling spree,
In this glassy world, laughter runs free.

The Enclosed Haven

Inside a bubble, the plants do sway,
Poking their heads to join the play.
A snail in shades, he takes a stroll,
While broccoli whispers, "I'm on a roll!"

A tiny door leads to flights of dreams,
Where minty fairies dance in teams.
"Chive my way!" a radish does call,
In this quirky realm, we're having a ball.

Peeking through glass, a cat goes by,
With a curious look and a twitching eye.
"Can I join the fun?" it seems to plead,
But the peas just giggle, "Not at this speed!"

In this tiny world, all's a blend,
Where laughter and greenery never end.
Each leaf a jester, each bud a clown,
Their antics sure could lift any frown.

Breathe in the Radiance

Sunlight bounces off glassy walls,
While geraniums host giggle-filled balls.
The lavender struts with a fragrant flair,
While thyme tries to dance without a care.

Bumbles buzz around like they own the place,
"Excuse me, friend, that's my flower space!"
A tulip chuckles, its petals aflame,
Breezy puns are its favorite game.

Amidst the glass, a frog takes a leap,
Into a pool full of secrets to keep.
"Can you keep a secret?" it croaks with delight,
"This lily may glow more than just at night!"

And so they sway, these playful things,
In this wee world where joy surely springs.
With laughter and love, let's wiggle and sway,
In this absurd haven, we'll have our day!

Memory of the Rainforest

A whisper of green in the humid air,
Laughter of leaves in a playful flair.
Mosquitoes excuse themselves with grace,
As a wayward lizard joins the race.

Vines hang low, like a toddler's art,
Snaking 'round pots like they own the part.
"Let's swing!" shouts the ivy with glee,
While orchids nod, "They are just so free!"

In the glassy home, a monkey's grin,
With a cheeky wiggle, it jumps right in.
Fish out of water? No, just fine in glass,
They swim through laughter with a splish and a splash.

With sunshine bursting and whimsy alive,
Every sprout here knows just how to thrive.
Jokes in this jungle make the heart soar,
In this tropical realm, who could ask for more?

Beneath the Crystal Canopy

Beneath a dome, the flowers giggle,
In a sunlit bowl, their laughter wiggles.
A tomato speaks to a fragile rose,
"Why are we here? Nobody knows!"

Bees wear shades, buzzing with flair,
Butterflies dance without a care.
A cucumber lies, claiming it's spry,
"I'm the real veggie, just look at my tie!"

Amidst the glass, a snail takes a seat,
Sipping dew, feeling quite elite.
"Slow down for life, the wise ones say,
But in this place, I might just sway!"

So underneath this shiny veil,
Nature's antics never fail.
With each twist, every snicker and grin,
Life's a riot within this skin.

Enclosed in Bloom

In this wacky world of leafy fame,
A carrot yells, "I'm the one to blame!"
For the weeds that giggle and tease all day,
"We're just here for a bit of play!"

The daisies wear hats, oh what a sight,
While the radishes pout, feeling contrite.
"We want the spotlight, not just the shade!"
Squeaks the broccoli, feeling betrayed.

A grape joked, "I'm just here to wine,
Cracking up under the vine.
Let's toast to our roots, we're quite the crew,
In this bouncy bubble of morning dew!"

Laughter erupts, that's the key,
In this vibrant place, full of glee.
So join the fun, take off that frown,
In our world of bloom, wear your crown!

Whispered Secrets of the Verdant Dome

In the heart of the dome, secrets share,
A peony whispers, filled with dare.
"Did you hear the tale of the sprouting seed?
It thought it was a flower, but wanted to lead!"

Underneath the glass, whispers abound,
With thyme and basil gossiping all around.
"Did you see how the mint so slyly threaded?
He claimed he was 'fresh', but really, he dreaded!"

A radish chuckled, "I'm really quite hot,
But as a root, I'm stuck on my spot!"
"Don't fret my friend, you're the toast of the town,
You might find your groove, just look around!"

So, secrets dance upon this vine,
In laughter's embrace, all will be fine.
For beneath the glass where the whimsy flows,
Even the shyest bloom joyfully shows.

Glass Petals and Morning Dew

In the bright of morn, the petals gleam,
A daffodil winks, fulfilling a dream.
"I'm a star!" she says, in the day's early light,
While peas in the peapods giggle with delight.

A fern does a jig, flapping its fronds,
"I'm the king of this jungle, I'm making my bonds!"
Spring onions whisper, plotting their scheme,
"Let's plant ourselves in a juicy theme!"

Beneath the glass, a riot ensues,
Foliage frolics and shares good news.
"Let's start a band, a jam on a whim,
With jazzed-up roots, and flowers that swim!"

So gather around, let's dance to the beat,
In this glassy place, life tastes so sweet.
With laughter and fun, and nature's delight,
We'll bloom forever in morning's soft light.

The Hidden Oasis

In corners tucked with gentle cheer,
Plants giggle softly, never fear.
A turtle's charm, a gnome's sly grin,
Who knew the fun that sprouted within?

With each little bloom, a joke unfurls,
Petals like giggles, oh how they twirl!
The sunbeams dance, casting silly sights,
While frogs recite their late-night flights.

Lizards play tag on the glassy dome,
While ants debate if this is home.
A breeze tickles leaves, they shake with glee,
In this wacky world, come laugh with me!

Butterflies chuckle, flit and prance,
In this glass place they love to dance.
Oh, what a sight, such folly to see,
A hidden oasis, come join the spree!

Fragile Landscapes

With soil that's soft and dreams that sprout,
A weathervane sings and shouts.
Dandelions wear crowns of gold,
In this fragile world, stories unfold.

The moss is thick, a squishy bed,
Where ladybugs dance, and chatter's widespread.
A pot of thyme gives sage advice,
Just sprinkle laughter, not too precise!

Sunlit leaves, a comic show,
Bubbles of laughter in the flow.
A grape vine jokes, "I'm getting stuck!"
As squirrels pass by, they start to pluck.

Within the glass, hilarity grows,
Plants with puns that only they know.
A fragile haven, don't look too fast,
In this funny world, joy is amassed!

Shimmering Safe Haven

In twinkling pots, the mischief thrives,
Tiny critters wearing high-fives.
A minty breeze whispers jokes so light,
While vines laugh softly, what a sight!

A cactus dressed in shiny beads,
Claims he's a star who dances with weeds.
The daisies snicker with bloom so bright,
Kudos, dear friends, for their silly height!

Beneath this lid, the humor flows,
While beetles boast of wacky shows.
A guardian wall of glassy glow,
Keeps in the fun as breezes blow!

Giggling stems and leaves in the fun,
A shimmering haven, joy's just begun.
Step right in, don't be late to the chase,
In this quirky haven, you'll find your place!

Blossoms Behind the Shield

Amidst the glass, a laughter spree,
Rosebuds debate as they sip their tea.
Sunflowers wink with golden glee,
"Who's the fairest?" they coax mischievously!

The pot-bellied frog dons a hat,
And croaks a tale of a scaredy cat.
With leafy friends and twinkling eyes,
Each petal holds secrets, all in disguise!

In corners suspicious, shadows play,
Whispers of blooms as they frolic away.
With feathery friends in the winged troupe,
They joke about the gardener's hoop!

Through the glass shield, a comedy blooms,
With blossoms laughing in fragrant rooms.
Join the fun, no need to conceal,
In this wild ballet, we laugh and heal!

Nature's Portrait in Glass

In a jar where plants reside,
Silly crickets try to hide.
Ladybugs wear tiny hats,
Dancing 'round with lazy rats.

Sunlight spills like lemonade,
While the ants have formed a parade.
Bees in top hats buzz with glee,
Throwing parties under the tree.

Squirrels peeking through the pane,
Claiming this their favorite lane.
Photosynthesis gone awry,
As leaves wave with a cheeky sigh.

And if the glass should crack one day,
The plants will stomp and shout hooray!
They'll frolic free from all that glare,
And laugh as they lose garden fare.

A Haven of Verdant Whispers

Within this dome of leafy cheer,
Parrots gossip, loud but clear.
Cacti wear their spiky clothes,
While orchids tease with petal shows.

Lizards lounge on sunny rocks,
Clad in very trendy frocks.
Bumblebees do somersaults,
In a world where no one halts.

A gopher shimmies, steals a snack,
A hidden stash tucked in a crack.
While the geraniums, bold and bright,
Join in laughter, oh what a sight!

With each bloom, a story's told,
Of wild adventures, brave and bold.
A kooky clan where nature plays,
In whispers soft, without delays.

Timeless Blooms in Transparent Silence

In a bubble of flourishing grace,
Rabbits hop in a slow-paced race.
Petunias giggle, stretch and yawn,
Under a rosy, sapphire dawn.

Frogs in tuxedos sing off-key,
While the daisies tease a bee.
Worms in spectacles, wise and quaint,
Plot their mischief as saints.

Sunflowers wink with golden cheer,
And trade jokes as the night draws near.
The moon stifles a dreamy grin,
As potted plants begin to spin.

The glass encases laughter bright,
In stillness holds the sheer delight.
So let them dream, these floral friends,
For the humor never ends.

Boundless Beauty Held at Bay

Behind this pane, the wonders prance,
As mushrooms join a silly dance.
Tulips twirl, wear smiles so wide,
While others slip, then take a slide.

Gnomes with hats that touch the sky,
Compete to see who's spry on fly.
Wind-blown petals play tag explore,
Laughing as they drift from shore.

Charming weeds, with tricks to play,
Sprout uninvited every day.
And though trapped in this gleaming case,
They find mischief, leave a trace.

For what's a life confined in glass,
Without a giggle, without sass?
So here they bloom, let merriment flow,
In a glassy realm where silliness grows.

www.ingramcontent.com/pod-product-compliance
Lightning Source LLC
Chambersburg PA
CBHW050304120526
44590CB00016B/2490